THEY LEFT, GOING THROUGH GALILEE.
JESUS, WHERE ARE WE GOING?
I WANTED TO SPEAK TO YOU ALONE.
LISTEN CAREFULLY.
THE SON OF MAN IS GOING TO BE BETRAYED.
BETRAYED INTO THE HANDS OF MEN, WHO WILL KILL HIM.
HE WILL BE BURIED, AND ON THE THIRD DAY WILL RISE, ALIVE.
THEY CONTINUED TRAVELING AROUND GALILEE, COMING TO CAPERNAUM, WHERE THEY WERE WELCOMED.
WHAT DID HE MEAN, "KILL HIM"?
MANY PEOPLE WANT HIM DEAD, IS HE SAYING THEY'LL SUCCEED?
I'M NOT GOING TO ASK HIM, ARE YOU?
EXCUSE ME!
I'M THE COLLECTOR OF THE TWO-DRACHMA TAX.
I KNOW YOUR TEACHER IS A GREAT, WISE MAN, BUT...
DOES HE PAY THE TEMPLE TAX?
OF COURSE HE DOES!
DOESN'T HE?
INSIDE, BEFORE PETER COULD EVEN ASK ABOUT IT, JESUS SPOKE.
PETER, A QUESTION.
WHO DO KINGS ON EARTH COLLECT TAXES FROM?
THEIR OWN SONS, OR THE SONS OF OTHERS?

MATTHEW 17:22-25; MARK 9:30-32; LUKE 9:43-45

FROM OTHERS.
YES, AND THE SONS ARE EXCUSED.
BUT WE DO NOT WANT TO OFFEND THEM, SO GO...
"TAKE A FISHING LINE TO THE WATER."
"CAST IN YOUR LINE."
"THE FIRST FISH YOU CATCH..."
"...OPEN ITS MOUTH."
FOUR DRACHMAS!
"PAY YOUR TAX AND MINE."
HERE YOU GO, SIR...

JESUS STAYED AROUND GALILEE, BECAUSE SOME IN JUDEA STILL WANTED TO KILL HIM.
THERE HE IS.
THE FEAST OF SHELTERS, CELEBRATED IN JERUSALEM, WAS NEAR AND JESUS' BROTHERS FOUND HIM.
JESUS, COME TO JUDEA, SO THEY CAN SEE YOUR MIRACLES!
DON'T DO THINGS IN SECRET.
THE WORLD DOES NOT HATE YOU, BUT IT HATES ME BECAUSE I TESTIFY TO ITS EVIL.
SO I MUST ONLY GO WHEN THE TIME IS RIGHT.
HIS OWN BROTHERS DON'T BELIEVE HIM.
JESUS STAYED IN GALILEE FOR THE TIME, CONTINUING HIS TEACHING AND HEALING.
THE WAY I SEE IT, PETER AND ANDREW ARE POSSIBLY THE GREATEST OF US.
AND THEN ME AND YOU.
WELL, ME AND THEN YOU, YOU MEAN.
NO, I SAID WHAT I MEANT...

MATTHEW 18:1; MARK 9:33; LUKE 9:46; JOHN 7:1-9

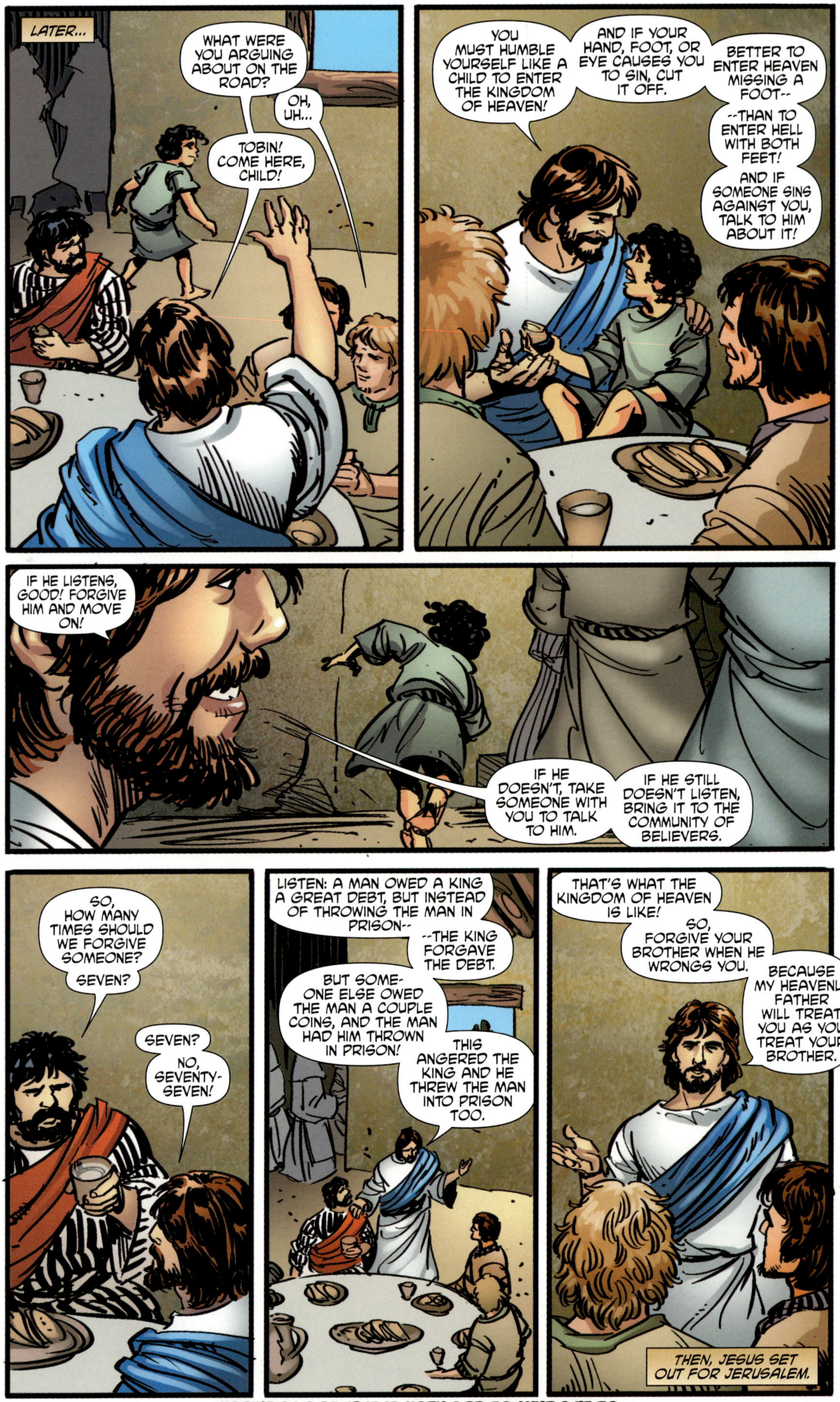
LATER...
WHAT WERE YOU ARGUING ABOUT ON THE ROAD?
OH, UH...
TOBIN! COME HERE, CHILD!
YOU MUST HUMBLE YOURSELF LIKE A CHILD TO ENTER THE KINGDOM OF HEAVEN!
AND IF YOUR HAND, FOOT, OR EYE CAUSES YOU TO SIN, CUT IT OFF.
BETTER TO ENTER HEAVEN MISSING A FOOT--
--THAN TO ENTER HELL WITH BOTH FEET!
AND IF SOMEONE SINS AGAINST YOU, TALK TO HIM ABOUT IT!
IF HE LISTENS, GOOD! FORGIVE HIM AND MOVE ON!
IF HE DOESN'T, TAKE SOMEONE WITH YOU TO TALK TO HIM.
IF HE STILL DOESN'T LISTEN, BRING IT TO THE COMMUNITY OF BELIEVERS.
SO, HOW MANY TIMES SHOULD WE FORGIVE SOMEONE? SEVEN?
SEVEN? NO, SEVENTY-SEVEN!
LISTEN: A MAN OWED A KING A GREAT DEBT, BUT INSTEAD OF THROWING THE MAN IN PRISON--
--THE KING FORGAVE THE DEBT.
BUT SOMEONE ELSE OWED THE MAN A COUPLE COINS, AND THE MAN HAD HIM THROWN IN PRISON!
THIS ANGERED THE KING AND HE THREW THE MAN INTO PRISON TOO.
THAT'S WHAT THE KINGDOM OF HEAVEN IS LIKE!
SO, FORGIVE YOUR BROTHER WHEN HE WRONGS YOU.
BECAUSE MY HEAVENLY FATHER WILL TREAT YOU AS YOU TREAT YOUR BROTHER.
THEN, JESUS SET OUT FOR JERUSALEM.

MATTHEW 9:2-35, 18:15-17; MARK 9:33-50; LUKE 9:47-50

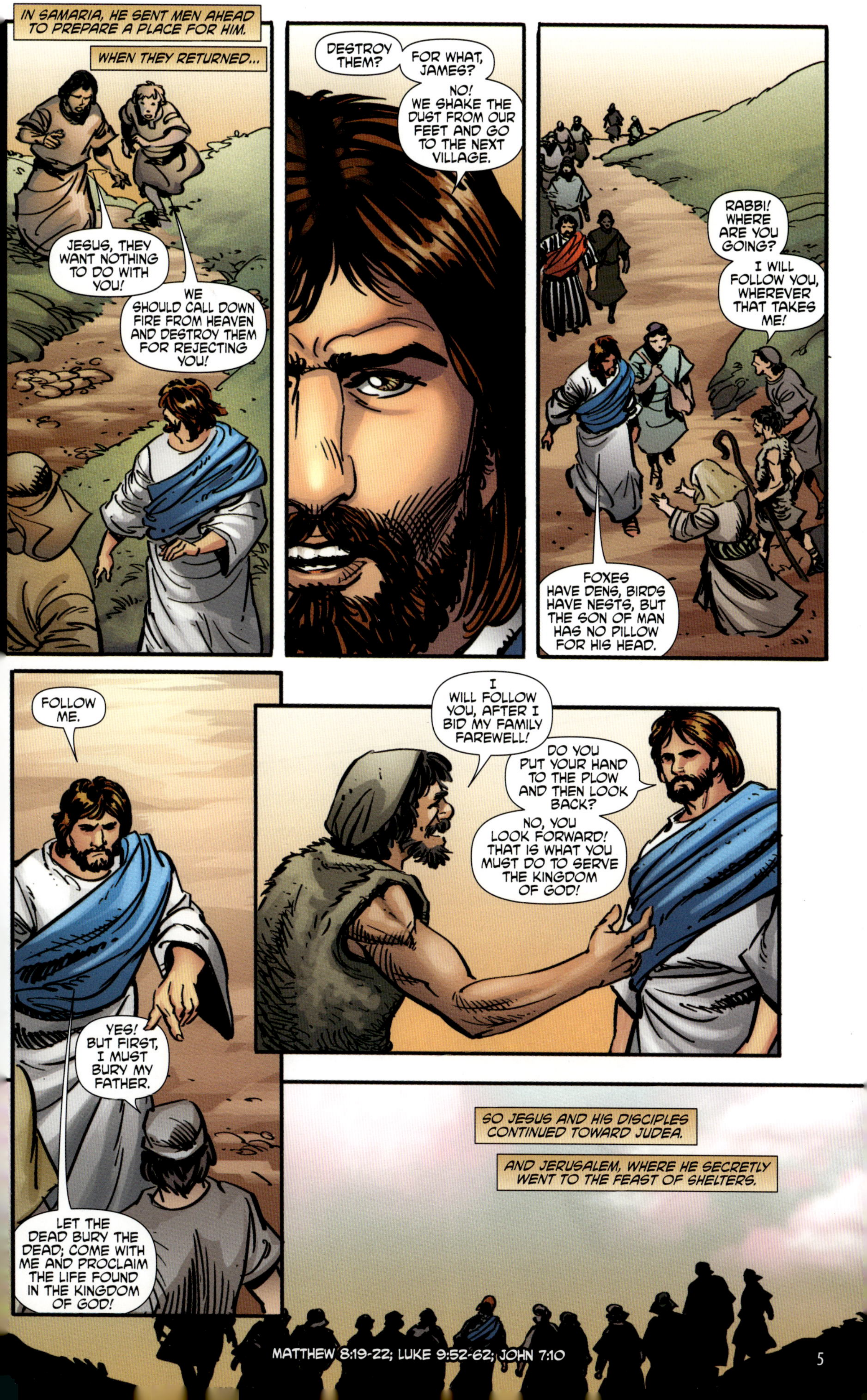
IN SAMARIA, HE SENT MEN AHEAD TO PREPARE A PLACE FOR HIM.
WHEN THEY RETURNED...
JESUS, THEY WANT NOTHING TO DO WITH YOU!
WE SHOULD CALL DOWN FIRE FROM HEAVEN AND DESTROY THEM FOR REJECTING YOU!
DESTROY THEM?
FOR WHAT, JAMES?
NO! WE SHAKE THE DUST FROM OUR FEET AND GO TO THE NEXT VILLAGE.
RABBI! WHERE ARE YOU GOING?
I WILL FOLLOW YOU, WHEREVER THAT TAKES ME!
FOXES HAVE DENS, BIRDS HAVE NESTS, BUT THE SON OF MAN HAS NO PILLOW FOR HIS HEAD.
FOLLOW ME.
YES! BUT FIRST, I MUST BURY MY FATHER.
LET THE DEAD BURY THE DEAD; COME WITH ME AND PROCLAIM THE LIFE FOUND IN THE KINGDOM OF GOD!
I WILL FOLLOW YOU, AFTER I BID MY FAMILY FAREWELL!
DO YOU PUT YOUR HAND TO THE PLOW AND THEN LOOK BACK?
NO, YOU LOOK FORWARD! THAT IS WHAT YOU MUST DO TO SERVE THE KINGDOM OF GOD!
SO JESUS AND HIS DISCIPLES CONTINUED TOWARD JUDEA.
AND JERUSALEM, WHERE HE SECRETLY WENT TO THE FEAST OF SHELTERS.

MATTHEW 8:19-22; LUKE 9:52-62; JOHN 7:10

MANY DIFFERENT PEOPLE WATCHED FOR JESUS IN JERUSALEM, EXPECTING HIM TO COME TO THE FEAST.
...I HEAR HE'S A GOOD MAN!
NO, HE'S JUST A GOOD LIAR!
HALFWAY THROUGH THE FEAST'S FESTIVITIES, JESUS MADE HIMSELF KNOWN.
HOW CAN YOU HAVE SUCH LEARNING WITHOUT HAVING STUDIED LIKE THE OTHER RABBIS?
MY TEACHING IS NOT MINE!
IT COMES FROM THE ONE WHO SENT ME!
IF YOU DO GOD'S WILL, YOU WILL SEE WHERE MY TEACHINGS COME FROM!
ISN'T THIS JESUS THE ONE THEY WANT TO KILL?
THEY AREN'T SAYING A WORD TO HIM WHILE HE TEACHES!
MAYBE THEY THINK HE'S THE CHRIST NOW!
IF YOU ARE THIRSTY, COME TO ME AND DRINK!
IF YOU BELIEVE IN ME, LIVING WATER WILL FLOW FROM YOU!
THIS GUY'S A PROPHET!
NO! HE'S THE CHRIST!
THE CHRIST ISN'T SUPPOSED TO COME FROM GALILEE!

JOHN 7:11-43

WE SENT GUARDS TO ARREST THIS JESUS, BUT EVEN THEY WERE DECEIVED BY HIS WORDS.
THE PEOPLE ARE DIVIDED.
HE KEEPS TEACHING. EVERY DAY.
HOW DO WE STOP HIM?
OUR LAW DOES NOT ALLOW US TO CONDEMN WITHOUT FIRST FINDING OUT WHAT HE'S DOING.
NICODEMUS, PROPHETS DO NOT COME FROM GALILEE!
I HAVE AN IDEA...
THE NEXT MORNING.
...HE WHO SENT ME IS TRUE!
YOU DO NOT KNOW HIM, BUT I DO BECAUSE HE SENT ME!
TEACHER!
TEACHER, THIS WOMAN WAS FOUND COMMITTING ADULTERY!
THE LAW OF MOSES TELLS US TO STONE SUCH AS HER!
WHAT SAY YOU?
WHAT ARE WE TO DO, TEACHER?
TELL US!
WHAT DOES "THE ONE WHO SENT YOU" SAY?

JOHN 7:28-29, 45-8:6

YES. STONE HER.
AND LET THE ONE WHO IS WITHOUT SIN CAST THE FIRST STONE.
WHERE DID EVERYONE GO?
IS THERE NO ONE HERE TO CONDEMN YOU?
NO ONE, SIR.
THEN NEITHER DO I.
GO, NOW. AND SIN NO MORE.
LEAVE THAT SINFUL LIFE BEHIND YOU!
YES, SIR! I WILL!
JOHN 7:7-11

THE NEXT TIME JESUS SPOKE TO THE PEOPLE...
I AM THE LIGHT OF THE WORLD.
IF YOU FOLLOW ME, YOU WILL NEVER WALK IN THE DARKNESS.
INSTEAD YOU WILL HAVE THE LIGHT OF LIFE!
YOUR TESTIMONY HAS NO WEIGHT!
YOU ARE YOUR OWN WITNESS!
MY TESTIMONY IS CREDIBLE.
THE LAW SAYS YOU NEED THE TESTIMONY OF TWO MEN.
I HAVE THAT.
ME.
AND THE FATHER, WHO SENT ME.
ADMIT IT!
YOU ARE A SAMARITAN!
AND A DEMON-POSSESSED ONE, AT THAT!
NO.
I HONOR MY FATHER, AND YOU DISHONOR ME!
ABRAHAM, YOUR FORE-FATHER, REJOICED AT THE THOUGHT OF SEEING MY DAY COME!
AND HE SAW IT!
AND WAS GLAD!
YOU'RE NOT EVEN FIFTY!
BUT YOU CLAIM TO HAVE SEEN ABRAHAM?
I SAY TO YOU--
--BEFORE ABRAHAM WAS BORN--
I AM!

JOHN 8:12-58

STONE HIM! THIS IS HERESY!
BUT--
IF YOU ARE A GOD-FEARING JEW--
--THEN PICK UP A STONE AND STONE HIM!

JOHN 8:59

PLEASE... HELP A MAN BLIND FROM BIRTH!
TEACHER, DID THIS MAN SIN OR DID HIS PARENTS?
THE PUNISHMENT MUST BE FOR HIS PARENTS, IF HE'S BEEN BLIND FROM BIRTH!
NO.
NEITHER.
THIS HAPPENED SO THAT GOD'S POWER COULD BE DISPLAYED IN HIM.
WHILE IT IS DAY, WE MUST DO THE WORK OF THE ONE WHO SENT ME.
WHEN NIGHT COMES, NO ONE CAN WORK.
WHILE I'M IN THE WORLD, I'M THE LIGHT OF THE WORLD.
PTOOOO
WHO'S THERE?
GO.
WASH THIS IN THE POOL OF SILOAM.
I... I...
LATER, AFTER THE BLIND MAN DID AS JESUS SAID--
HE SPOKE WITH AUTHORITY. WHO WAS HE?
I'VE HEARD HE'S CALLED JESUS.
JOHN 9:1-7

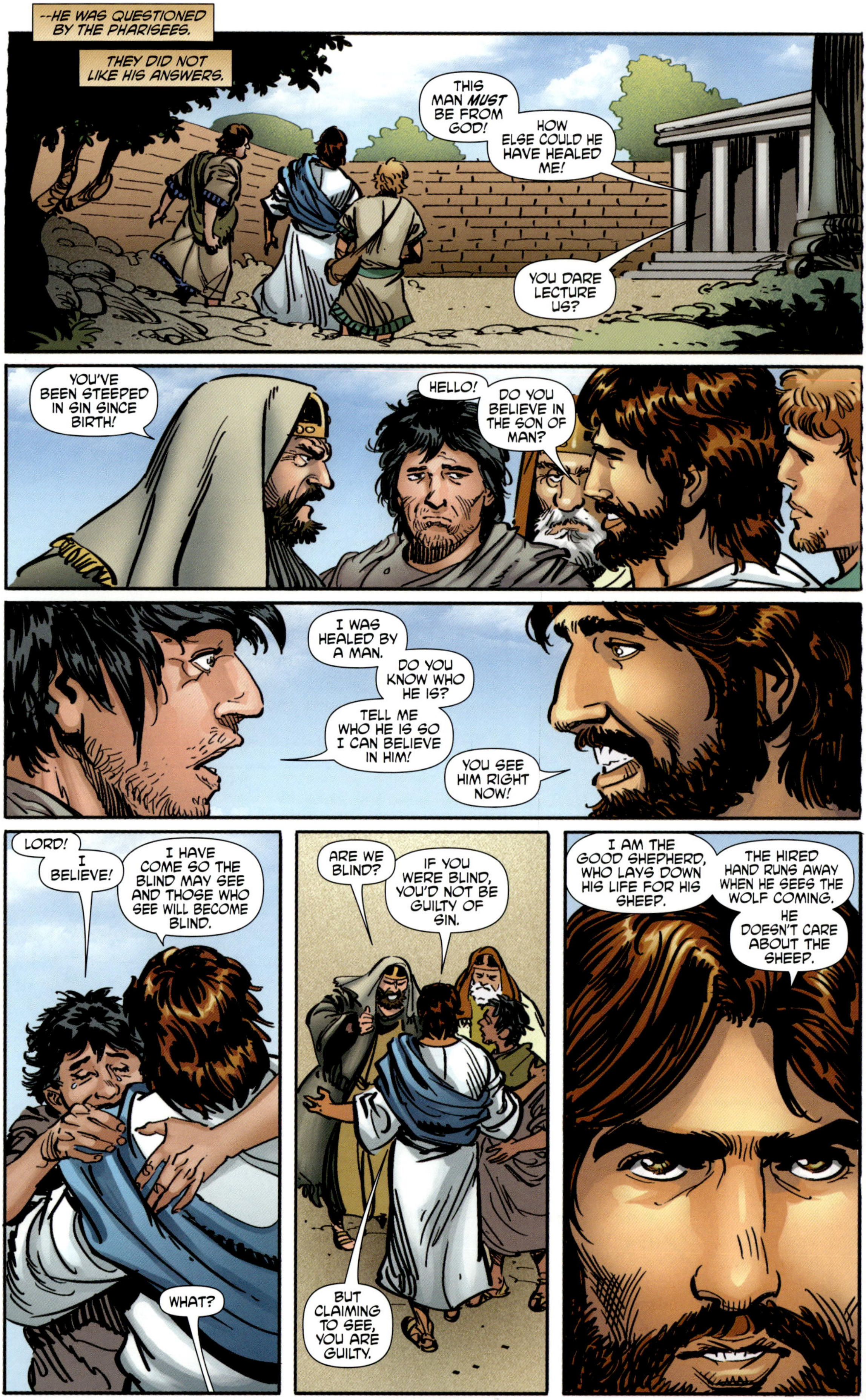
--HE WAS QUESTIONED BY THE PHARISEES.
THEY DID NOT LIKE HIS ANSWERS.
THIS MAN MUST BE FROM GOD!
HOW ELSE COULD HE HAVE HEALED ME!
YOU DARE LECTURE US?
YOU'VE BEEN STEEPED IN SIN SINCE BIRTH!
HELLO!
DO YOU BELIEVE IN THE SON OF MAN?
I WAS HEALED BY A MAN.
DO YOU KNOW WHO HE IS?
TELL ME WHO HE IS SO I CAN BELIEVE IN HIM!
YOU SEE HIM RIGHT NOW!
LORD!
I BELIEVE!
I HAVE COME SO THE BLIND MAY SEE AND THOSE WHO SEE WILL BECOME BLIND.
WHAT?
ARE WE BLIND?
IF YOU WERE BLIND, YOU'D NOT BE GUILTY OF SIN.
BUT CLAIMING TO SEE, YOU ARE GUILTY.
I AM THE GOOD SHEPHERD, WHO LAYS DOWN HIS LIFE FOR HIS SHEEP.
THE HIRED HAND RUNS AWAY WHEN HE SEES THE WOLF COMING.
HE DOESN'T CARE ABOUT THE SHEEP.

JOHN 9:8-10:13

AS A GOOD SHEPHERD, I KNOW MY SHEEP.
AND MY SHEEP KNOW ME!
AND I LAY DOWN MY LIFE FOR MY SHEEP!
NO ONE TAKES IT FROM ME. I GIVE MY LIFE VOLUNTARILY.
I HAVE AUTHORITY TO LAY IT DOWN.
AND AUTHORITY TO TAKE IT BACK UP.
THIS COMES FROM MY FATHER.
HE'S A MADMAN!
HE'S DEMON-POSSESSED! WHY WOULD ANYONE LISTEN TO HIM?
CAN A DEMON HEAL A BLIND MAN'S EYES?
AROUND THIS TIME, JESUS SPOKE TO SEVENTY-TWO FOLLOWERS, GIVING THEM A MISSION TO:
GO!
I SEND YOU OUT LIKE LAMBS AMONG WOLVES!
WHEN YOU ENTER A TOWN AND ARE WELCOMED, EAT WHAT IS PUT IN FRONT OF YOU.
HEAL THE SICK AND PREACH TO THEM THAT THE KINGDOM OF GOD IS NEAR.
IF YOU ARE NOT WELCOMED, GO OUT IN THE STREETS, WIPING THE DUST FROM YOUR SHOES--
JOHN 10:14-21; LUKE 10:1-11

WHOEVER LISTENS TO YOU LISTENS TO ME!
WHOEVER REJECTS YOU REJECTS ME!
AND WHOEVER REJECTS ME REJECTS THE ONE WHO SENT ME!
WHEN THEY RETURNED...
IT WAS AMAZING, JESUS!
EVEN THE DEMONS SUBMITTED TO US IN YOUR NAME!
MY FRIENDS, I SAW SATAN FALL LIKE LIGHTNING FROM HEAVEN.
I GAVE YOU AUTHORITY TO OVERCOME THE ENEMY!
BUT REJOICE, INSTEAD, THAT YOUR NAMES ARE WRITTEN IN HEAVEN!
FATHER, I PRAISE YOU BECAUSE YOU HIDE THESE THINGS FROM THE WISE AND EDUCATED--
--AND REVEAL THEM TO THE CHILD!
ONLY THE FATHER TRULY KNOWS THE SON.
AND THE FATHER IS ONLY KNOWN BY THE SON--
--AND THOSE TO WHOM THE SON CHOOSES TO REVEAL HIM.
LATER, SPEAKING TO THE TWELVE ALONE, JESUS SAID:
BLESSED ARE YOUR EYES!
FOR PROPHETS AND KINGS LONGED TO SEE AND HEAR WHAT YOU HAVE.
BUT THEY DID NOT!
LUKE 10:12-24

ONE DAY, AN EXPERT IN THE LAW TRIED TO TEST JESUS:
RABBI, A QUESTION!
WHAT MUST I DO TO GET ETERNAL LIFE?
WHAT DOES THE LAW OF MOSES SAY?
"LOVE THE LORD YOUR GOD WITH ALL YOUR HEART, SOUL, STRENGTH, AND MIND."
YES.
AND "LOVE YOUR NEIGHBOR AS YOURSELF."
YES! DO THAT AND YOU WILL LIVE!
BUT WHO IS MY NEIGHBOR?
LET ME TELL YOU A STORY.
A TRAVELER WAS ATTACKED AND ROBBED--
--AND LEFT FOR DEAD.
A PRIEST CAME ALONG, PASSING HIM BY.
A TEMPLE ASSISTANT DID THE SAME.
BUT A SAMARITAN SAW HIM AND TOOK PITY.
HE HELPED HIM TO SAFETY AND PAID FOR HIS CARE.
SO WHO WAS THE NEIGHBOR?
THE ONE WHO SHOWED HIM MERCY.
EXACTLY.
SO GO NOW AND DO THE SAME.
LUKE 10:25-37

JUST OUTSIDE BETHANY, A TOWN NEAR JERUSALEM.
JESUS! HELLO!
JESUS, YOU AND YOUR DISCIPLES PLEASE REST AND EAT IN MY HOME!
MY BROTHER LAZARUS AND SISTER MARY AND I WOULD BE HONORED!
WE WOULD BE DELIGHTED!
GREETINGS, JESUS!
WELCOME! THANK YOU FOR ACCEPTING MARTHA'S INVITATION!
IS THERE ANYTHING ELSE I CAN GET YOU BEFORE I BRING OUT THE MEAL?
NO, MARTHA, I THANK YOU.
MARY, I COULD USE YOUR HELP.
YES. IN A MOMENT.

LUKE 10:38-39

"A MOMENT" LATER...
WHERE IS SHE?
THERE'S SO MUCH TO DO!
WELL, THAT'S NOT RIGHT!
...IT IS NOT JUST YOUR ACTIONS, BUT YOUR HEART...
LORD!
TELL MARY TO HELP ME!
DON'T YOU CARE THAT SHE'S MAKING ME DO ALL THE WORK BY MYSELF?
MARTHA, YOU'RE WORRIED AND UPSET ABOUT MANY SMALL THINGS.
ONLY ONE THING IS WORTH WORRYING ABOUT.
MARY KNOWS THAT, AND THAT WILL NOT BE TAKEN FROM HER.

LUKE 10:39-42

ANOTHER DAY, AFTER JESUS HAD GONE OFF TO PRAY.
LORD, WOULD YOU TEACH US TO PRAY?
LIKE JOHN THE BAPTIST TAUGHT HIS DISCIPLES?
YES.
WHEN YOU PRAY, SAY:
OUR FATHER.
YOUR NAME IS HOLY.
MAY YOUR KINGDOM COME.
WE ASK YOU FOR THE FOOD WE NEED.
AND WE ASK YOU FOR FORGIVENESS OF OUR SINS--
--AS WE FORGIVE THOSE WHO SIN AGAINST US.
AND DON'T LET US GIVE IN TO TEMPTATION.
ASK AND IT WILL BE GIVEN; SEEK AND YOU WILL FIND; KNOCK AND THE DOOR WILL BE OPENED.
FOR IF A SON ASKS FOR A FISH, WHAT FATHER WOULD GIVE HIM A SNAKE?
OR IF AN EGG IS ASKED FOR, WHAT FATHER WOULD GIVE HIS SON A SCORPION?
IF YOU'RE EVIL, AND STILL KNOW HOW TO GIVE GOOD GIFTS--
--SURELY YOUR HEAVENLY FATHER WILL GIVE THE HOLY SPIRIT TO THOSE WHO ASK!

LATER...
JESUS! I KNOW YOU HAVE HEALED MANY!
PLEASE, HEAL MY FRIEND!
HE CANNOT SPEAK!
HE'S POSSESSED!
THAT'S WHY HE'S MUTE!
NOT FOR LONG...
I COMMAND THE DEMON AFFLICTING THIS MAN--
--DEPART FROM HIM!
TH-- TH--
THANK YOU...

LUKE 11:14

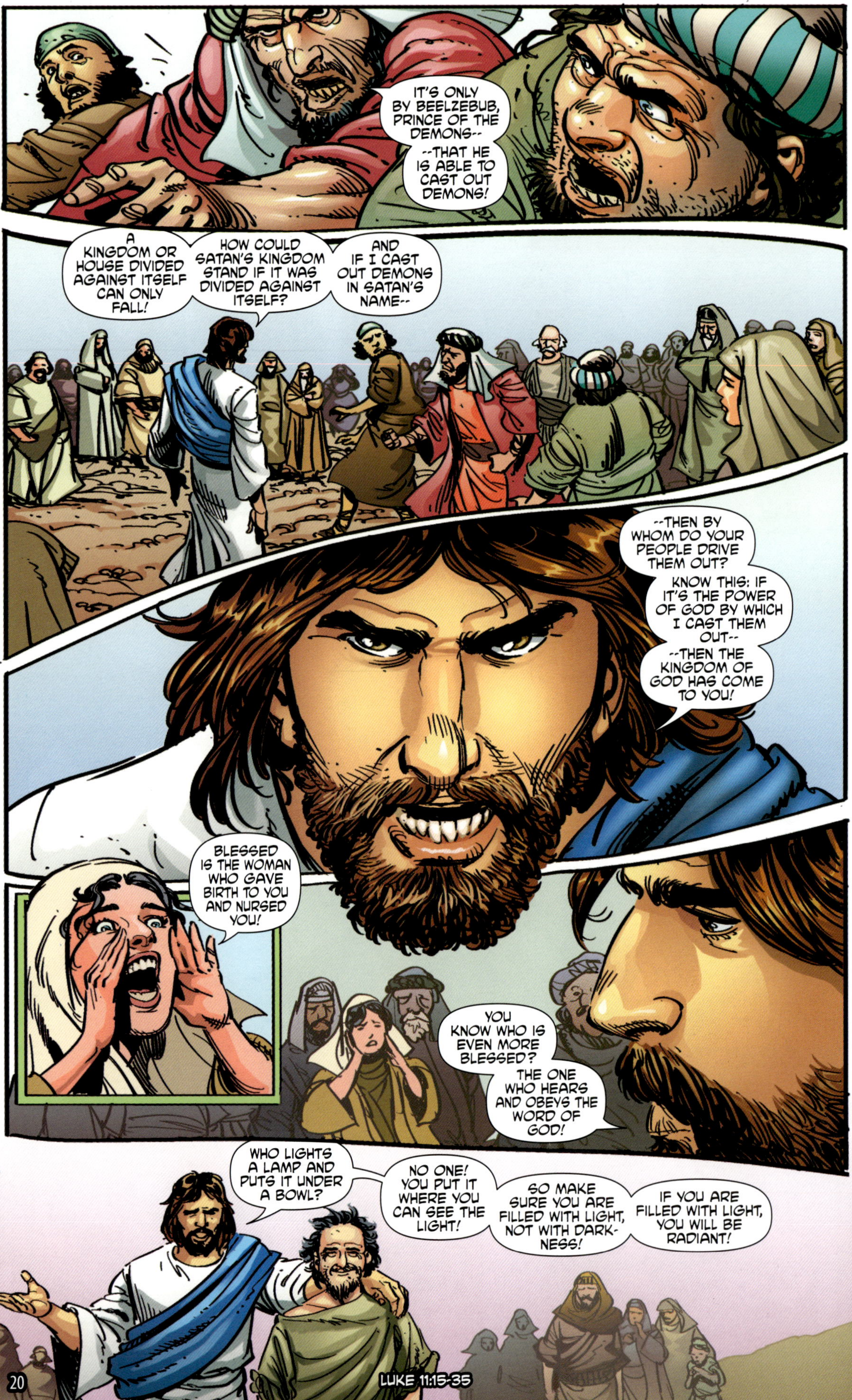
IT'S ONLY BY BEELZEBUB, PRINCE OF THE DEMONS--
--THAT HE IS ABLE TO CAST OUT DEMONS!
A KINGDOM OR HOUSE DIVIDED AGAINST ITSELF CAN ONLY FALL!
HOW COULD SATAN'S KINGDOM STAND IF IT WAS DIVIDED AGAINST ITSELF?
AND IF I CAST OUT DEMONS IN SATAN'S NAME--
--THEN BY WHOM DO YOUR PEOPLE DRIVE THEM OUT?
KNOW THIS: IF IT'S THE POWER OF GOD BY WHICH I CAST THEM OUT--
--THEN THE KINGDOM OF GOD HAS COME TO YOU!
BLESSED IS THE WOMAN WHO GAVE BIRTH TO YOU AND NURSED YOU!
YOU KNOW WHO IS EVEN MORE BLESSED?
THE ONE WHO HEARS AND OBEYS THE WORD OF GOD!
WHO LIGHTS A LAMP AND PUTS IT UNDER A BOWL?
NO ONE! YOU PUT IT WHERE YOU CAN SEE THE LIGHT!
SO MAKE SURE YOU ARE FILLED WITH LIGHT, NOT WITH DARK-NESS!
IF YOU ARE FILLED WITH LIGHT, YOU WILL BE RADIANT!

AFTER HE FINISHED SPEAKING...
RABBI, WOULD YOU PLEASE COME AND SUP WITH ME TONIGHT?
THANK YOU FOR COMING.
I HAVE MANY QUESTIONS.
AND I KNOW YOU HAVE MANY ANSWERS!
YOU... YOU DIDN'T WASH YOUR HANDS.
HOW CAN YOU NOT WASH YOUR HANDS?
YOU PHARISEES...
YOU CLEAN THE OUTSIDE OF THE DISH.
BUT INSIDE YOU ARE FULL OF GREED AND WICKEDNESS!
FOOLS! DIDN'T GOD MAKE BOTH YOUR FLESH AND YOUR SOUL?

LUKE 11:37-41

BUT IF YOU'D LEARN TO GIVE AWAY WHAT'S INSIDE THIS DISH TO THE POOR--
--YOU'D BE CLEAN!
WOE TO YOU.
SORROW WILL COME TO YOU BECAUSE YOU MAKE SURE TO GIVE A TENTH OF YOUR HERB GARDENS TO GOD!
YOU TITHE, BUT YOU FORGET GOD'S LOVE AND JUSTICE.
AND YOU COVET THE BEST SEATS IN THE SYNAGOGUES!
YOU ARE LIKE UNMARKED GRAVES THAT MEN WALK OVER WITHOUT EVEN KNOWING!
DO YOU KNOW YOU INSULT US SAYING SUCH THINGS?
WOE TO YOU, BECAUSE YOU LOAD PEOPLE DOWN WITH LAWS AND RULES--
--AND THEN DON'T HELP THEM CARRY THE LOAD!
WOE TO YOU, BECAUSE YOU HAVE TAKEN AWAY THE KEY TO KNOWLEDGE.
SO YOU YOURSELVES DON'T GO THROUGH THE DOOR.
AND YOU DON'T LET ANYONE ELSE ENTER EITHER.
HOW DARE YOU?
AND BY WHOSE AUTHORITY DO YOU SAY SUCH THINGS?
WHAT HAPPENED IN THERE?
BE CAREFUL!
DON'T LET THE HYPOCRISY OF THE PHARISEES GET INTO YOU, TOO!

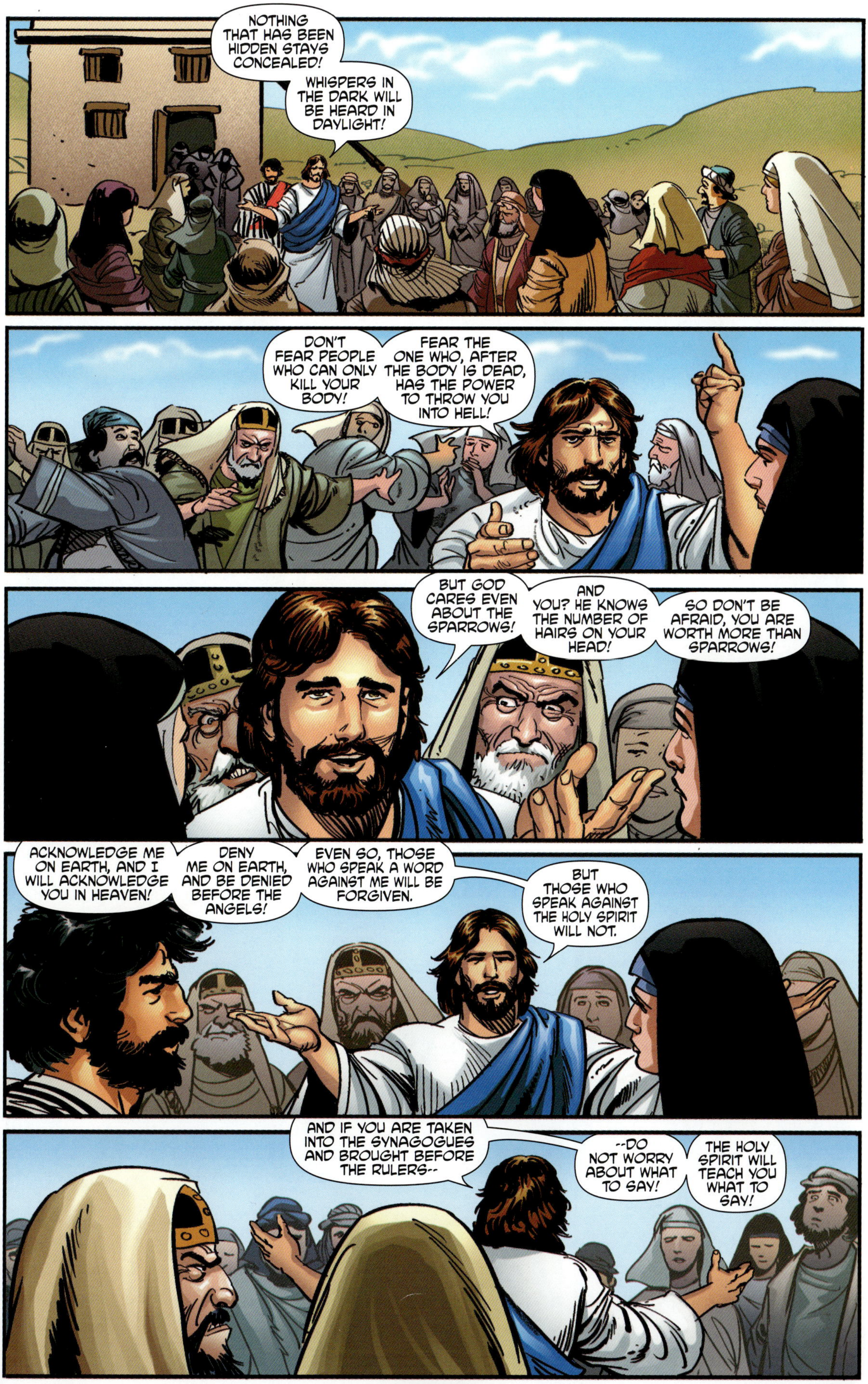
NOTHING THAT HAS BEEN HIDDEN STAYS CONCEALED!
WHISPERS IN THE DARK WILL BE HEARD IN DAYLIGHT!
DON'T FEAR PEOPLE WHO CAN ONLY KILL YOUR BODY!
FEAR THE ONE WHO, AFTER THE BODY IS DEAD, HAS THE POWER TO THROW YOU INTO HELL!
BUT GOD CARES EVEN ABOUT THE SPARROWS!
AND YOU? HE KNOWS THE NUMBER OF HAIRS ON YOUR HEAD!
SO DON'T BE AFRAID, YOU ARE WORTH MORE THAN SPARROWS!
ACKNOWLEDGE ME ON EARTH, AND I WILL ACKNOWLEDGE YOU IN HEAVEN!
DENY ME ON EARTH, AND BE DENIED BEFORE THE ANGELS!
EVEN SO, THOSE WHO SPEAK A WORD AGAINST ME WILL BE FORGIVEN.
BUT THOSE WHO SPEAK AGAINST THE HOLY SPIRIT WILL NOT.
AND IF YOU ARE TAKEN INTO THE SYNAGOGUES AND BROUGHT BEFORE THE RULERS--
--DO NOT WORRY ABOUT WHAT TO SAY!
THE HOLY SPIRIT WILL TEACH YOU WHAT TO SAY!

LUKE 12:2-12

RABBI! TELL MY BROTHER THAT THE RIGHT THING TO DO IS DIVIDE HIS INHERITANCE WITH ME!
I'M NOT YOUR REFEREE!
INSTEAD, I TELL YOU TO BE ON YOUR GUARD AGAINST GREED!
YOUR LIFE IS MORE THAN ACCUMULATING THINGS!
DO NOT WORRY ABOUT YOUR LIFE!
WHAT YOU'LL EAT, DRINK, OR WEAR!
LIFE IS MORE THAN THAT!
CONSIDER THE LILIES! THEY DON'T LABOR AND SPIN--
--BUT WAS SOLOMON IN HIS GREATEST SPLENDOR EVER CLOTHED LIKE THEM?
SEEK GOD'S KINGDOM, AND THE REST WILL COME TO YOU AS WELL!
WHERE YOUR TREASURE IS? THAT IS WHERE YOUR HEART IS.
WHEN YOU SEE A CLOUD RISING IN THE WEST YOU KNOW IT'S GOING TO RAIN.
WHEN THE WIND BLOWS FROM THE SOUTH, YOU KNOW IT WILL BE HOT.
YOU CAN INTERPRET THE SKY, BUT NOT THE SIGNS OF THE PRESENT TIMES!
YES! TERRIBLE TIMES!
PILATE HAD SOME GALILEAN TROUBLEMAKERS KILLED, MIXING THEIR BLOOD WITH THE PASSOVER SACRIFICES!
THOSE GALILEANS MUST HAVE BEEN TERRIBLE SINNERS TO MEET SUCH A FATE!
ACTUALLY, NO!
SIN IS SIN! UNLESS YOU REPENT, YOU WILL ALL PERISH!

LUKE 12:13-13:8

THE MAN BORN BLIND'S STORY

"TRIAL" John 9:1-41

I'VE TOLD MY STORY MANY TIMES.
ESPECIALLY IN THOSE FIRST DAYS, WHEN EVERYTHING I SAW WAS SOMETHING NEW!
SOMETHING EXCITING! WONDERFUL! BEAUTIFUL!
WE'VE BEEN TOLD YOU USED TO BEG IN THE STREETS, SAYING YOU WERE BLIND?
AND YET, HERE YOU ARE--
--ABLE TO SEE?
YES, SIR.
HOW? WERE YOU LYING? PRETENDING TO BE BLIND?
THE WITNESSES WHO BROUGHT THIS TO OUR ATTENTION CONFIRM HE WAS BLIND.
I WAS!
UNTIL JUST A SHORT TIME AGO, THAT IS.
SO WHAT HAPPENED?
THAT QUESTION HAS BEEN ASKED OF ME BY MANY PEOPLE.
SOME GENUINELY WANT TO KNOW.
OTHERS? WELL, THEY HAVE OTHER MOTIVATIONS.
MY PARENTS LED ME TO MY USUAL PLACE AND LEFT ME THERE, AS USUAL.
IT WAS THE SABBATH. PEOPLE TEND TO BE MORE GENEROUS ON THE SABBATH.
THEN I HEARD SOME VOICES--

"I REALIZED THEY WERE TALKING ABOUT ME."
RABBI, WHO SINNED?
WAS IT THIS MAN OR HIS PARENTS WHO SINNED THAT HE'D BE BORN BLIND?
"I'D HEARD THE QUESTION BEFORE IN THE PAST."
AND A GOOD QUESTION IT IS!
AS THE TALMUD SAYS, "HE PUNISHES THE SIN OF THE FATHERS TO THE THIRD AND FOURTH GENERATION!"
I BELIEVE A PERSON CAN SIN WITHIN THE WOMB, FOR HOW ELSE CAN YOU EXPLAIN--
ENOUGH!
THIS IS NOT THE TIME FOR THIS ARGUMENT!
PLEASE, CONTINUE.
SURE, RIGHT.
SO ANOTHER VOICE ANSWERED THEM. A GENTLE, AUTHORITATIVE VOICE.
NEITHER THIS MAN NOR HIS PARENTS.
IT WAS NOT SIN THAT CAUSED HIS BLINDNESS.
IT WAS SO THE MIGHTY WORK OF THE LORD COULD BE REVEALED ON THIS DAY!
"I HEARD HIM SPIT."
"NOT UNUSUAL. I'VE BEEN SPIT ON MORE TIMES THAN I CAN COUNT."
"BUT HE DIDN'T SPIT ON ME. INSTEAD, WELL..."
"HE TOUCHED MY EYES."

"COVERED THEM IN MUD."
"WE TALKED FOR A BRIEF MOMENT AND HE SAID:"
GO, NOW.
WASH IN THE POOL OF SILOAM.
"OF COURSE, I DID AS HE SAID!"
"AND WHEN THE MUD CAME FROM MY EYES--"
"--I WAS HEALED!"

MIXING DIRT INTO MUD? ON THE SABBATH?
OBVIOUSLY, THAT MAN IS NOT FROM GOD, OR HE WOULD NOT HAVE HEALED ON THAT DAY!
IF THIS MAN IS A SINNER, HOW COULD HE DO THIS THING?
THE PROPHETS SAY HEALING THE BLIND IS A SIGN OF THE MESSIAH'S COMING!
WHAT DO YOU SAY?
WHO WAS THIS MAN?
WELL, I DIDN'T SEE HIM! I WAS STILL BLIND WHEN HE COVERED MY EYES!
WHAT DO YOU KNOW ABOUT HIM?
I KNOW HE IS A PROPHET, AT THE VERY LEAST.
YOU DIDN'T SEE HIM, BUT WE ALL KNOW WHO YOU ARE TALKING ABOUT.
HE COULD HAVE HEALED YOU ON ANY OTHER DAY!
IF HE WAS NEVER BLIND IN THE FIRST PLACE, PERHAPS THIS JESUS SET IT UP!
WHAT, TWO DECADES AGO, JESUS TOLD THIS MAN'S PARENTS TO PRETEND THEIR BABY WAS BLIND?
SEND FOR HIS PARENTS! LET'S SEE WHAT THEY HAVE TO SAY!
YOU STAY PUT!
WE DON'T WANT YOU CORROBORATING YOUR STORIES!

IS THIS YOUR SON?
HE IS.
HE WAS.
AND HE WAS BORN BLIND?
I THINK WE CAN STOP THIS THREAD OF QUESTIONING.
EVERYONE WHO KNOWS HIM SAYS HE WAS BLIND FROM BIRTH.
IF HE WAS BORN BLIND--
--HOW, PRAY TELL, CAN HE SEE NOW?

I KNOW HE IS MY SON.
I KNOW HE WAS BORN BLIND.
BUT I DO NOT KNOW HOW HE CAN SEE NOW.
I DO NOT KNOW WHO OPENED HIS EYES.
YOU SHOULD ASK HIM!
HE'S OLD ENOUGH!
HE'S OF AGE!
GET THEM OUT OF HERE.
WE'LL CONTINUE THIS TOMORROW...
SON, WE'RE SORRY.
YOU UNDERSTAND, RIGHT?
IF WE SAID WE THOUGHT THAT JESUS PERSON HAD DONE THIS, WELL...
THE PHARISEES AND THE CHIEF PRIESTS DON'T LOOK KINDLY ON PEOPLE WHO TALK ABOUT JESUS.
I UNDERSTAND.
I DO.
"I WAS JUST GLAD THAT THE FIRST TIME I SAW THEM WAS NOT THIS DAY."
"WHEN I SAW THEM COWER IN FEAR INSTEAD OF DEFEND ME."